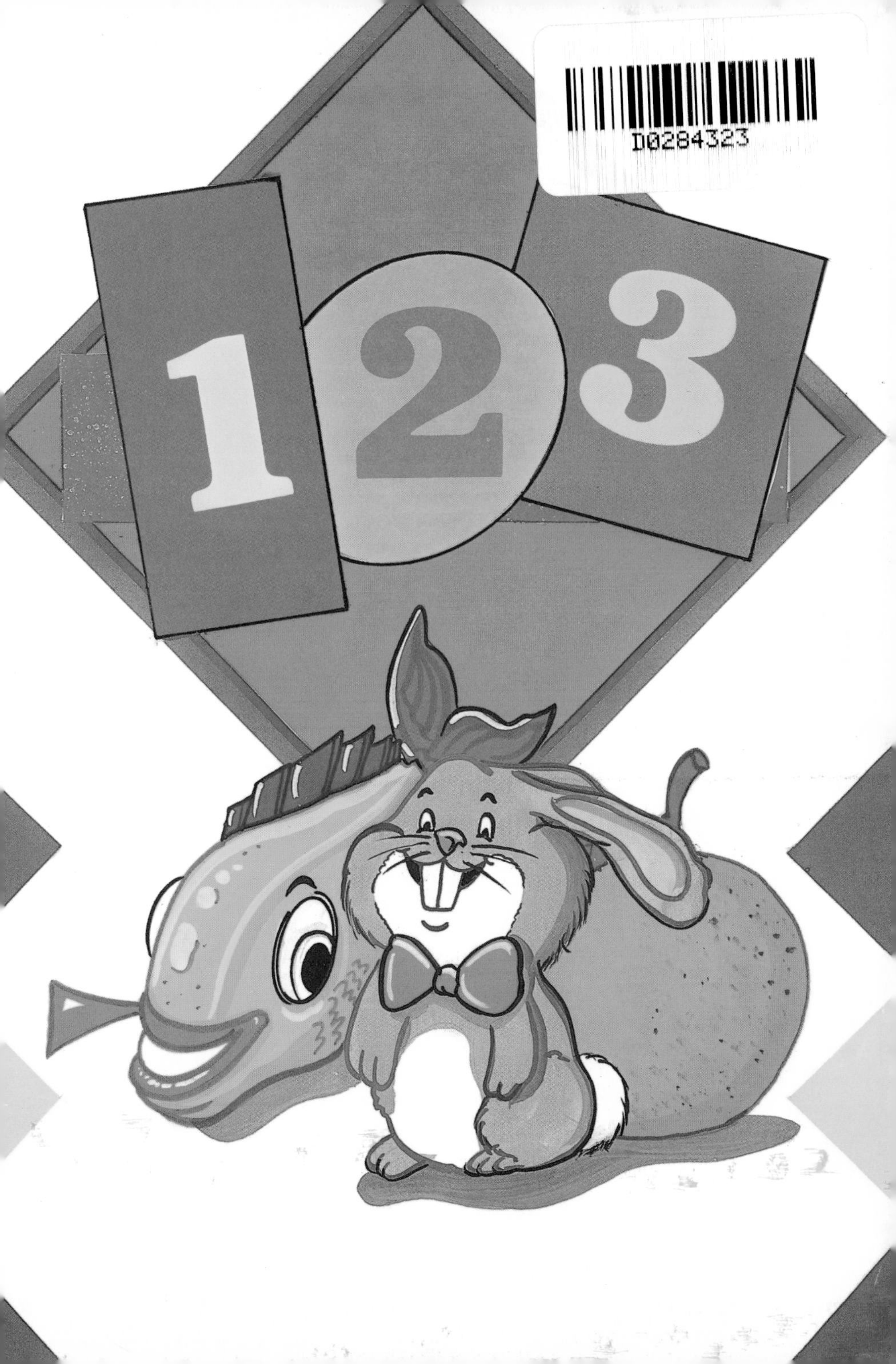
1 2 3

1

one seal

1

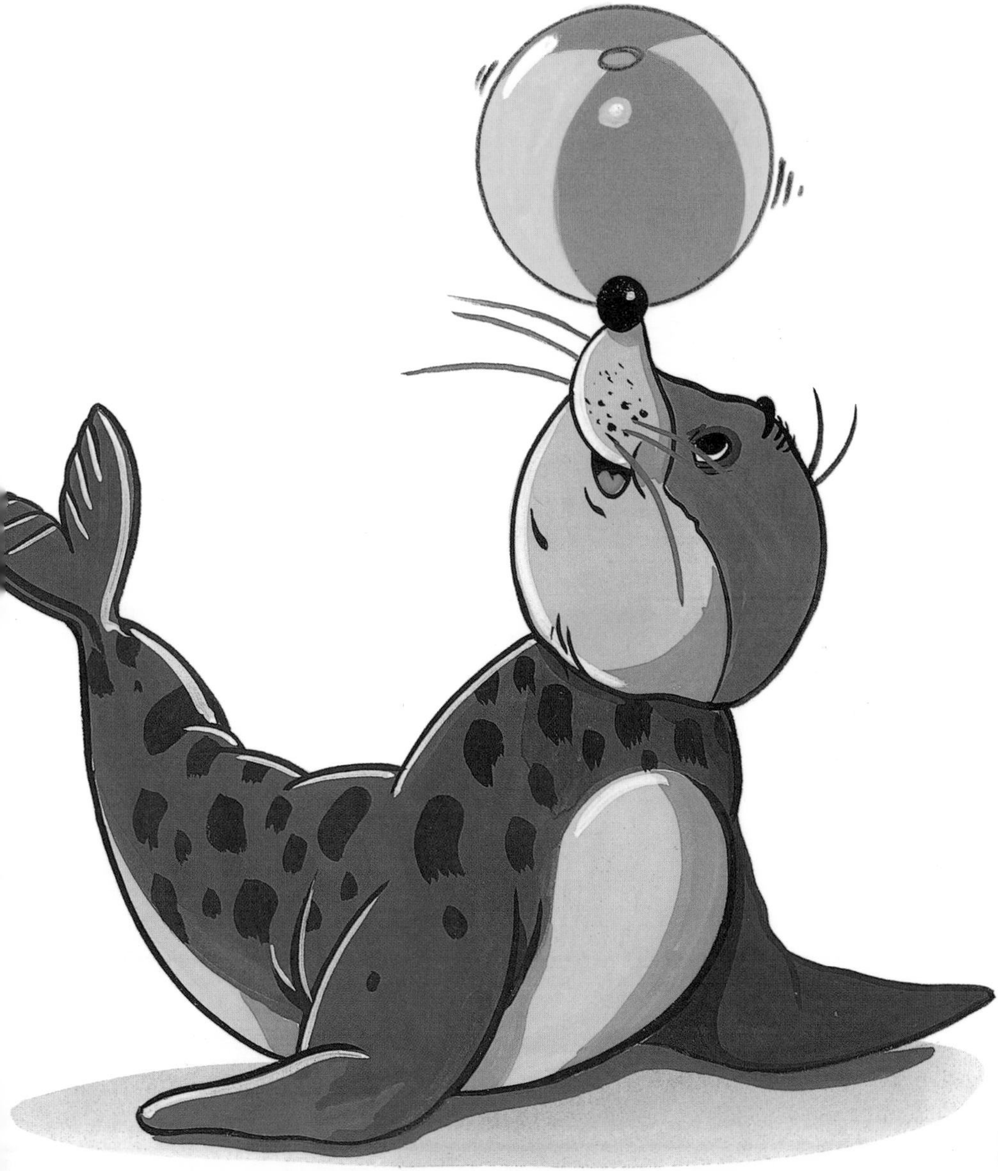

2

two cows

2

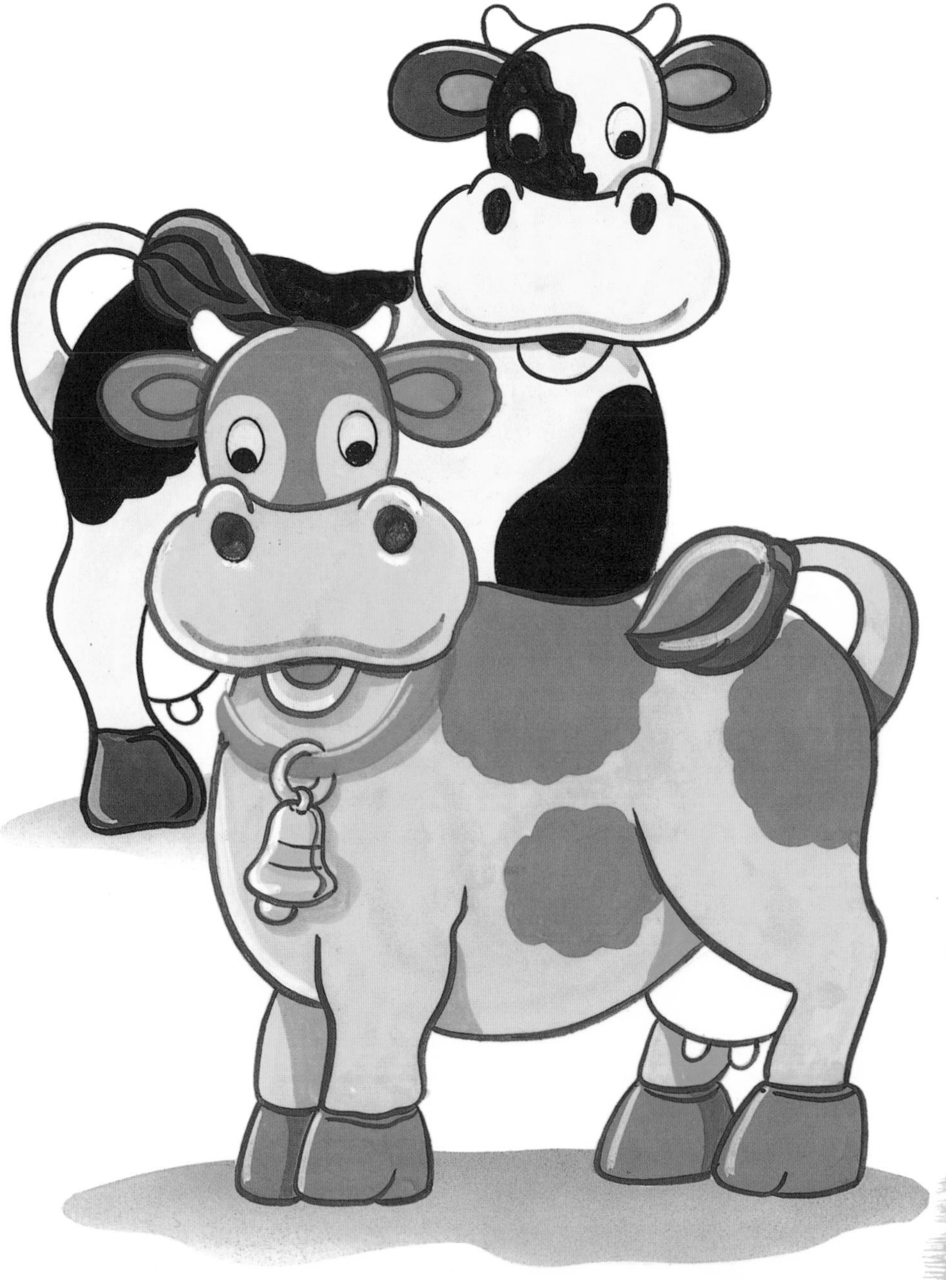

3

three fish

3

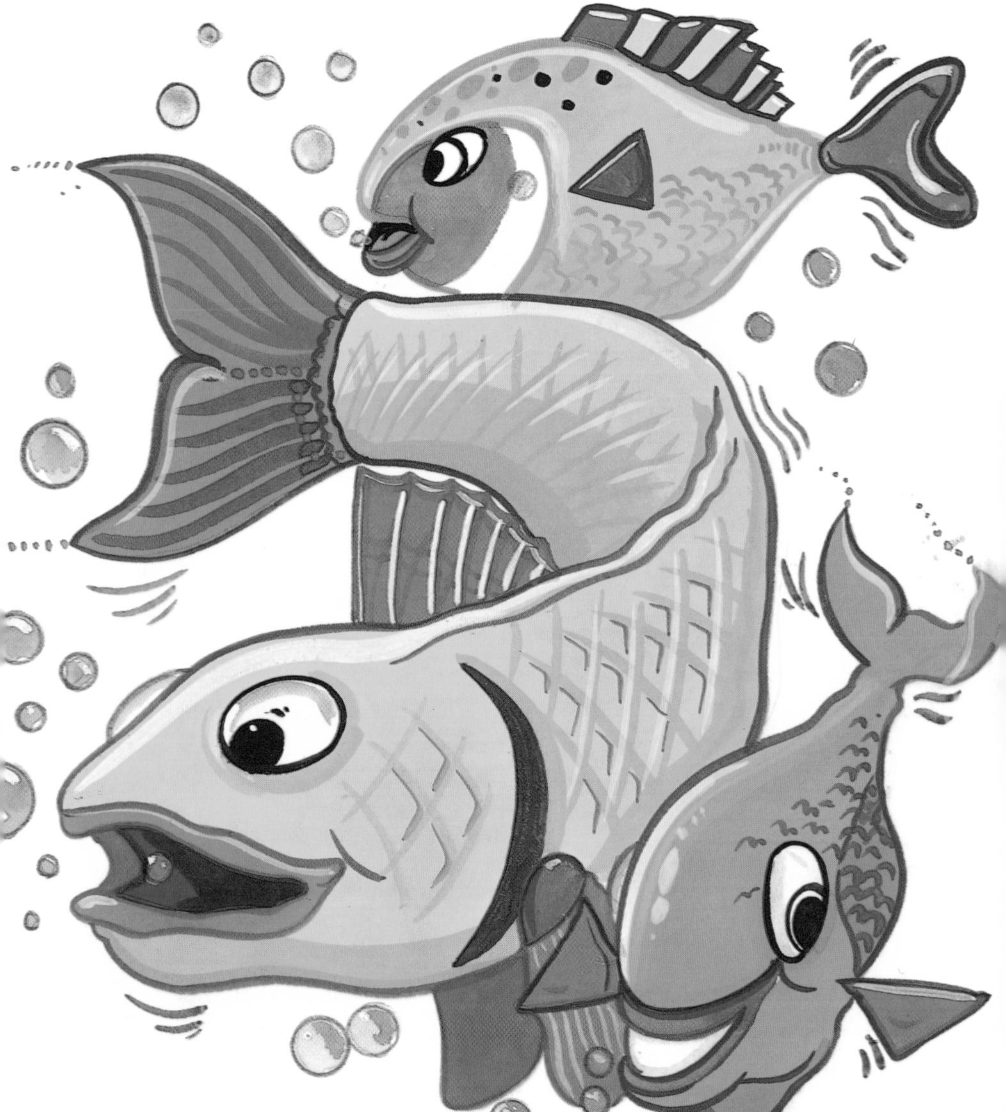

4

four balls

4

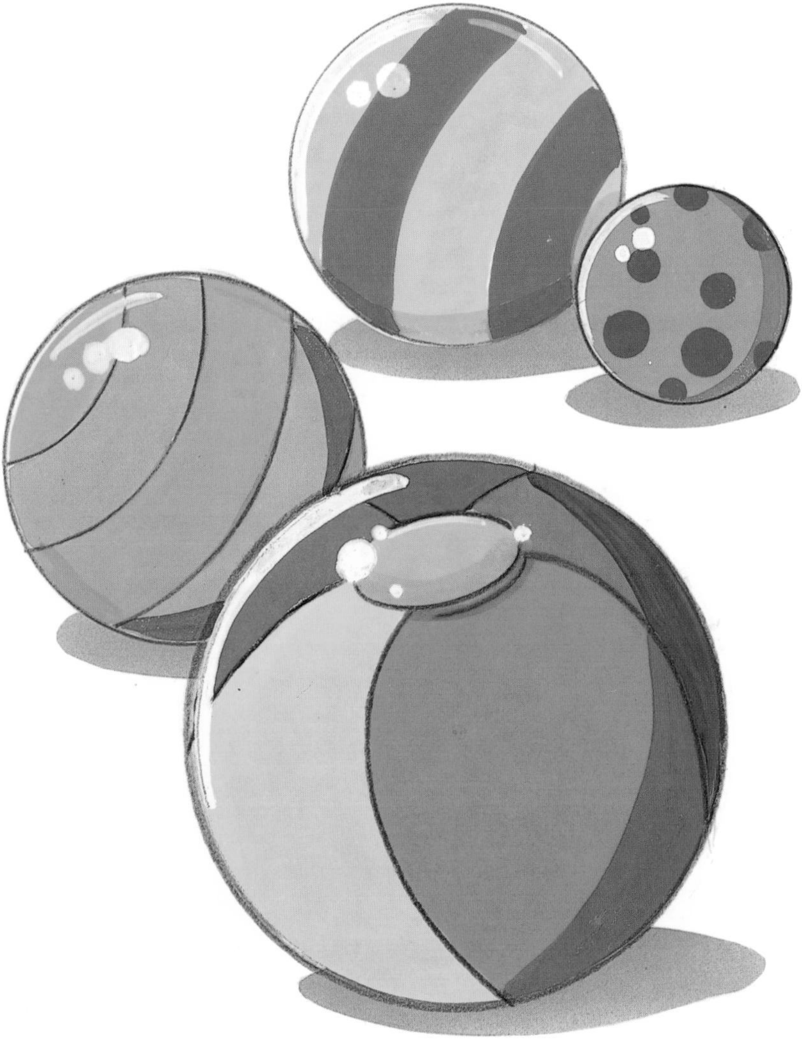

5

five
cherries

5

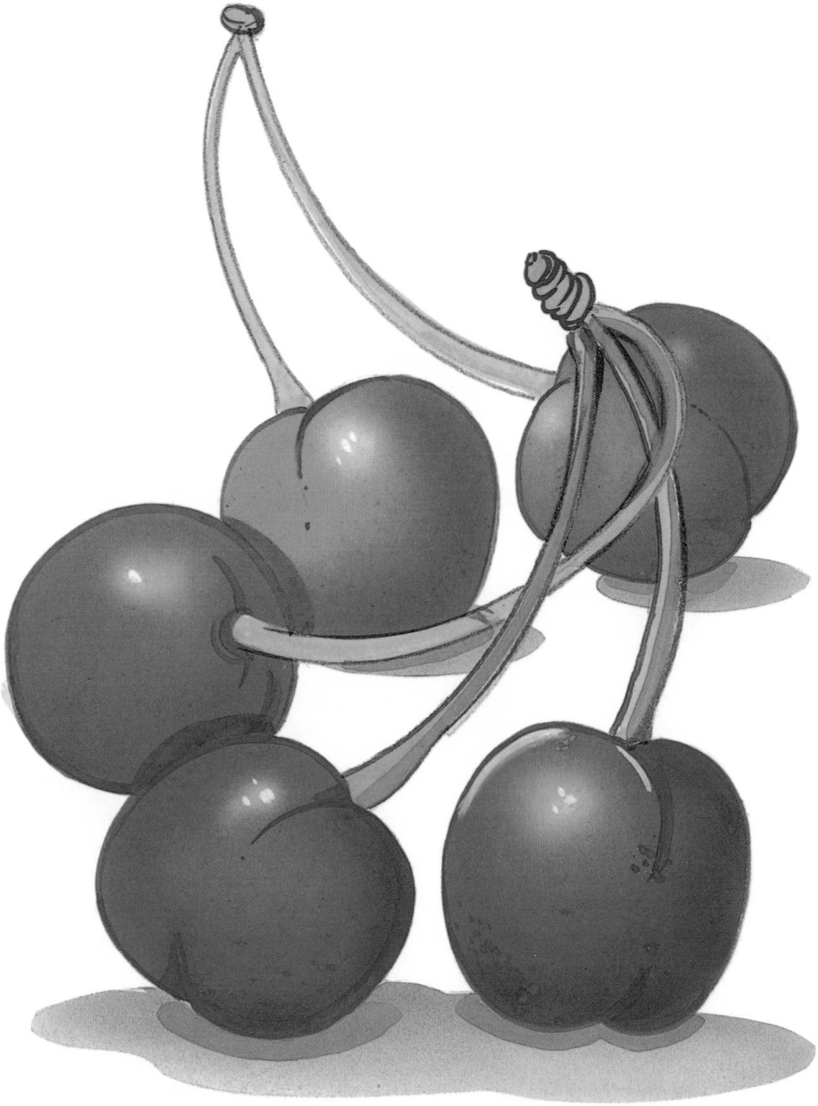

6

six dogs

6

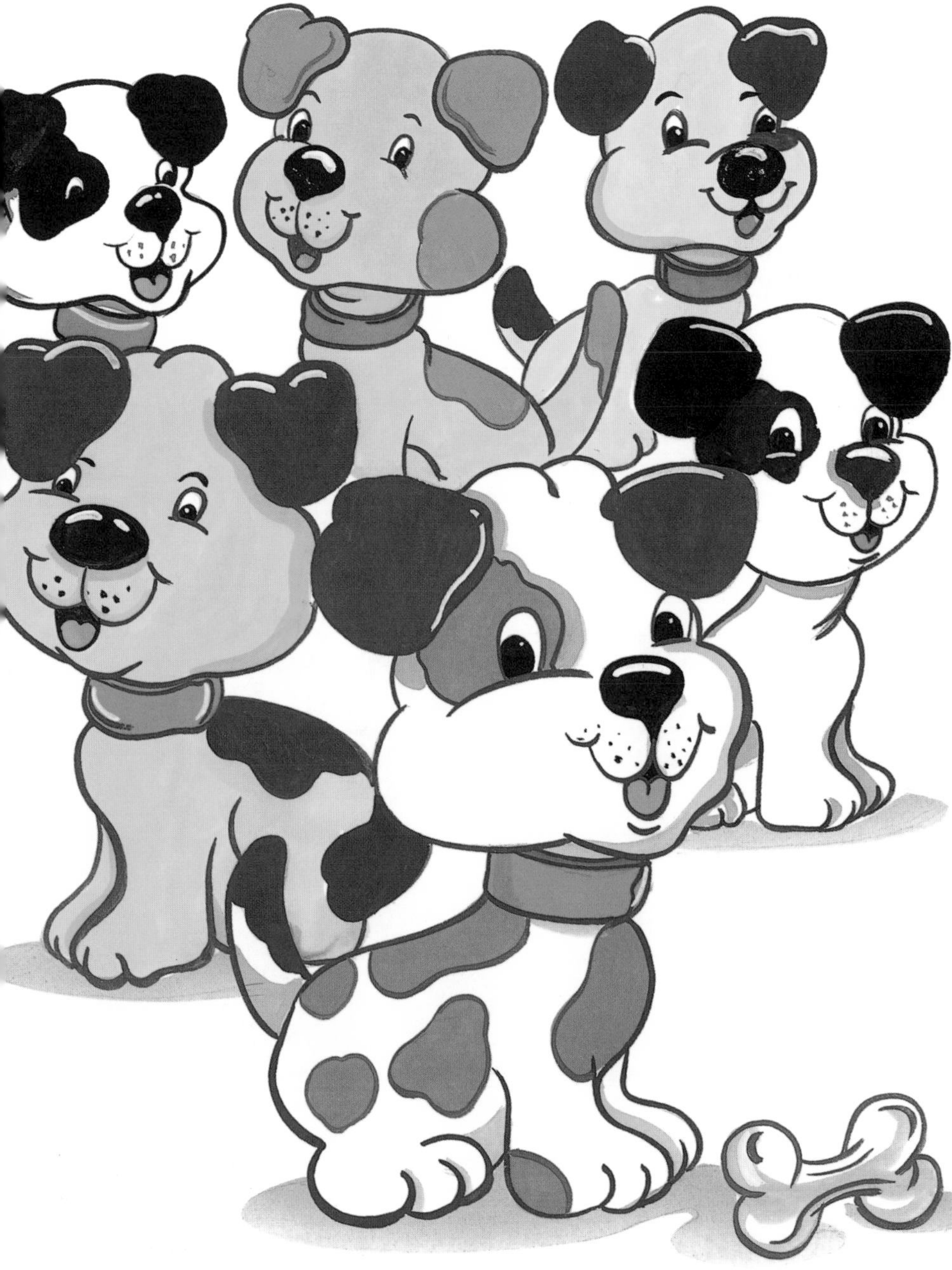

7

seven flowers

7

8

eight lollipops

8

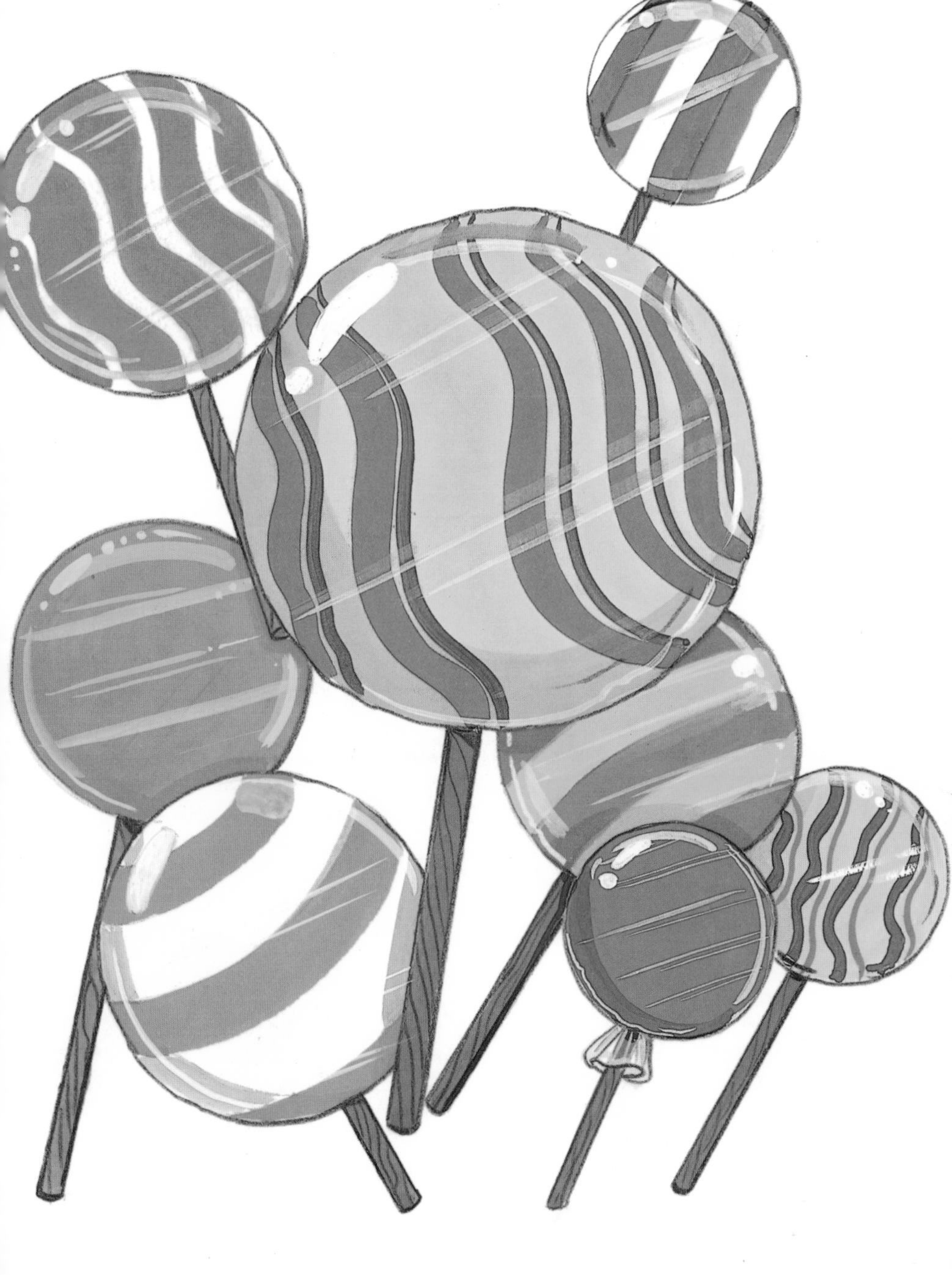

9

nine rabbits

9

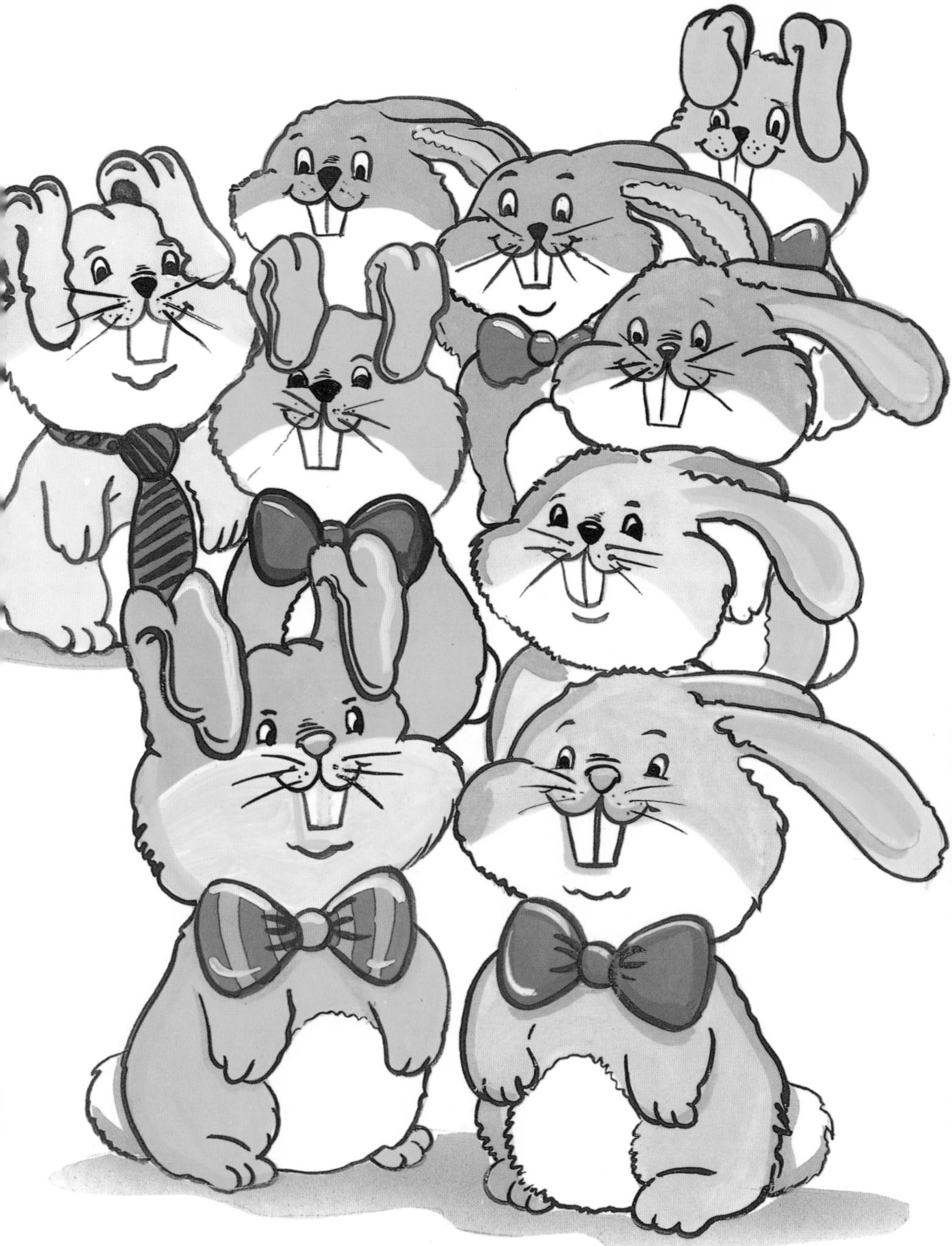

10

ten oranges

10